Cheryl;

I feel l... ....
was orchestrated. You
are "special". I love
You already. Enjoy the
Read.

I'M NOT THAT WOMAN!

PORTIA TAYLOR

Lift Bridge Publishing
Info@liftbridgepublishing.com
www.liftbridgepublishing.com

Book Cover: Morgan 4 Design
Editing: Critique Editing Services

Ordering Information: Quantity sales. Special discounts are avail-able on quantity purchases by corporations, associations, and others. For details, contact the publisher at the email above. Or-ders by U.S. trade bookstores and wholesalers.

Please contact Lift Bridge Publishing:
Tel: (888) 774-9917
Printed in the United States of America
Publisher's Cataloging-in-Publication data

Taylor, Portia.

ISBN 978-1-6425491-8-8

DEDICATION

This book is dedicated to every girl who has believed the lie that she has to take what life hands her and make the best of it. I challenge that. I say *MAKE LIFE*, don't take life and if you don't like the way you were born the first time, you can be born again.

Contents

FOREWORD

I'm Not That Woman by Portia Taylor would describe every woman at one time or another in her life. The world has tried to define us, tell us who we are, what we can do and what we can have. It's only when we discover the truth that we can honestly face the lie and declare, "I'm not that woman." The greatest discovery will be that of who God made you to be. Simply be you and do you. THIS BOOK will help you realize the things in your life that have shaped who you are today.

I have known Pastor Portia for many years and have watched her grow into this awesome woman of God, loving wife, mother and anointed pastor. You will discover a great awakening of who you are as you journey with Portia, discovering who she is. There are great women in the Bible who have paved the way of discovery for us. In *I'm Not that Woman* you will learn about women who were courageous, strong, fearless and of great faith. Women who faced their fears, rebuked them and accomplished God's perfect plan. God has a purpose and perfect plan for your life, and even if you don't feel perfect, God doesn't make mistakes. You are "fearfully and wonderfully made" with a unique anointing that will fulfill your destiny.

I discovered a glimpse of who God said we are in a dream many years ago. God commissioned me to go tell women "God has given you your place back." In short, the Lord was saying there is a place that we were given by God that was stolen way back in the Garden of Eden. A place of dominion, power and equality. I believe as you read *I'm Not That Woman,* you'll discover your place and get it back. You will recognize the voice of the enemy and discover the voice of your Heavenly Father.

The biggest crime in our society is "identity theft." Just like the enemy stole Adam's and Eve's identities in the garden, the enemy is trying to rob you of your true identity and redefine who you are through life's experiences and circumstances, so that you will not see the full manifestation of your potential (1 John 4:17). God is putting things in order so that your potential is not only realized but exercised. And it first starts with knowing who you are. Those circumstances don't define you, they are there to reaffirm to you who you really are, to bring out your strengths and faith in who God made you to be.

2 Corinthians 5:14-17 [Amplified Bible, (AMP)] really sums it up for us, "For the love of Christ controls and urges and impels us, because we are of the opinion and conviction that [if] One died for all, then all died; And He died for all, so that all those who live might live no longer to and for themselves, but to and for Him Who died and was raised again for their sake. Consequently, from now on we estimate and regard no one from a [purely] human point of view [in terms of natural standards of value]. [No] even though we once did estimate Christ from a human viewpoint and as a man, yet now [we have such knowledge of Him that] we know Him no longer [in terms of the flesh]. Therefore if any person is [ingrafted] in Christ (the Messiah) he is a new creation (a new creature altogether); the old [previous moral and spiritual condition] has passed away. Behold, the fresh and new has come!"

My prayer as you take this journey with Portia is that you will echo her declaration in this book and embrace the fresh and new life that was prearranged before the earth's foundation for you.

-Apostle Cynthia Brazelton, Pastor, Victory Christian Ministries International

ACKNOWLEDGEMENTS

I want to thank my husband, Demond Taylor for finding me early in life. Your voice has always pushed me to be a finisher. Thank you for reminding me that I am on the Best Sellers list and supporting me through this journey. You are my lover, my coach and my friend.

To my mom, Angie Hudson, my first and greatest example of a woman of God. It was secretly sitting outside your prayer closet where I first learned that I didn't have to be the woman this world was trying to make me. Your declaration of who I was opened a new possibility of living for me. I heard you. Thank you for seeing me.

To Apostle Cynthia Brazelton, global leader of the church that saved my life—Victory Christian Ministries International, for being a trailblazer, my mark, my first example of a great woman in ministry. Thank you for not giving up on your journey and not giving up on me, even when my skirt was too short ☺. Thank you for always being the standard and never compromising your position. I jokingly nicknamed you "Jesus," but you are one of His greatest examples in the Earth.

To my sister, Nikkie Knowles, thank you for being unfiltered, and for all your encouragement, your jokes when I needed them and most of all my "love notes" that you always send before I speak— "I am important, I am smart, I am kind!"

To my daughter Paris, you are my greatest inspiration. All my writings are for my baby girl. Thank you for constantly asking me when I would finish my books and coloring all my book covers to get me started. Mommy loves you.

To Mandy (Amanda) and Marcie (M&M), you guys started me on my blogging journey. Thank you for the late-night conversations pulling more out of me. Thanks for all the editing, the "Pastor P you can't say that or Pastor P you need to say that". Thank you for giving your life to make sure life was released to my readers.

To my Girls, my inner court, Thanks for true friend-ship. I pray others can have what we have. Thanks for letting me know when my "booty" was hanging out-CAN YOU SEE ME!? Love y'all.

To THE TEAM, Lift Bridge Publishing Company; you are more than a publishing company, thank you for your relentless approach and untiring work ethic. To Aye Waiter and Epiphany Enterprise; my creatives, thank you for tapping into gifts I didn't know were there. To Morgan 4 Design, for the best graphics and book cover, thank you for putting art to what I see.

To my subscribers, Y'ALL TOTALLY ROCK! Thank you for your feedback and continuing the conversations.

PREFACE

Who Am I? Portia Taylor. No, literally I am Portia. Throughout your reading I don't mind if you call me "P" in your head. You will have those moments when you just put down the book and say, "PPPPPPPPPPP! Did she really say that?" Or you may have a congregational moment when you just throw the book and holler, "Pastor!" And if you are from the urban side of the tracks you may have to fold down a few pages in your book, close it and say "Girl, bye" while you get yourself together and reassess what just happened. And for my conservative, less expressive sisters, you may simply clutch your pearls and clear your throat as you take a moment to regain your composure.

Throughout this book, you will meet me. My character, my voice, my strong desire to see you be who God ordained you to be. I like to think of myself as your confidant, the one you tell all your secrets to (because I really am a good listener and trust me, I know most of your secrets anyway). Then I give it to you straight—no chaser—come back and make sure you heard me while wiping your tears or stepping a little closer in your face, whichever you require.

I like to start, listen in on, and provoke conversations. My prayer is that for you this will be just that, a conversation. Together, we will have conversations with women who have gone on before us because I truly believe we can learn life lessons from great women of God who've won some and lost some. (Or so they thought. I believe there is absolutely nothing lost in the Kingdom.)

They have so much to say. Why do I believe such a thing? Because I talk to these great women of God regularly. I am inviting you into my world. I want to invite you to a place that goes beyond what is written, and to journey into conversations that most of us women want to have but haven't taken the opportunity. I am always down for "girl talk." I like to talk to Eve and Bathsheba. I talk to the loose Rahab and the lonely Leah, and I have always been the type of girl who can even kick it with some of the guys like Joshua (my prototype) and Paul. I tend to be a bit nosey, so I peep in on conversations that God has had with many of these people and will show you how God is often trying to get us to pull up and converse on a greater level.

I plan to share some of my own experiences and life lessons as well and maybe some of yours (depending on who's reading). Please don't get thrown off by my style; since the age of 15 it is how I have fallen in love with the Word of God. It is actually pretty entertaining. Just like Jesus spoke in parables to make a strong point, I will push the envelope. I have heard people say I am edgy. I am not edgy; I want to take you over the edge. I want it to be too much. Why? Because God invested too much for our freedom. He spared nothing. If you allow me to, I will show you things that will make you laugh, cry, question, share and read more.

So "Who is Portia?" you ask, the God's honest answer is I am still in discovery. We are all in discovery. We may be at different seasons in our lives, but the reality is we are all a part of a journey called discovery. If you open your eyes and incline your ears, you become aware that you are everywhere. I can identify with the little girl who wishes she had more hair and was lighter and be present with her insecurities. While also identifying with the woman who is a workaholic and desperately needs a break and to possibly even change professions but has to keep up the image of being a hard worker. I can see myself in Michelle Obama who didn't let anyone silence her as a young female, who was often misunderstood, but was determined to finish on top and became the First Lady of the United States. It's called ambition. I see myself pastoring thousands while still pastoring the one and at the same time making an impact in the Earth that ripples through generations. It's called calling. I am fully and completely present in the moment, yet I am living ready for the next unveiling of myself. I now realize there is no there. I always hear people say, "If I could just get there." There doesn't exist. There's only now. I have learned to enjoy here. It is the discovery of who I am that makes me declare who I am not.

As women we have said, "I'm Not That Woman," after hearing an unimaginable experience they watched someone else go through and silently thought, *That will never be me*. My declaration comes from a different place. It comes from having been that woman and realizing I believed a lie and empowered that lie. See, low self-esteem is a lie empowered. It came from not having a real revelation of the love of God; therefore, I could not love myself. As I discovered the lies, I grabbed on to the truth, but not just in theory. I experienced that truth and became free by the truth I now know. Listen, I am not speaking from the end of the process, rather from the middle. In discovery, the lies die and the truth is revealed daily. I am good with that.

So who is Portia? Right now, to be me is like the endless possibilities of being instead of the pressure of doing.

It's enjoying loving myself and my neighbor, understanding that I didn't choose my neighbor, rather they were placed in my life to show me another side of who I am and who God is. It's enjoying the freedom of choice in every moment. It's choosing living over dying, assurance over doubt, love over fear, focus over distraction, and expectation over complacency. It's finally living from a sure place—living out loud with self-expression. Knowing that myself is healthy and I am not just expressing a golden-calf version of myself. Many people live out loud from an unhealthy place. I have had a front row seat to unbalanced, unhealthy women in life. Yet, through my discovery I have learned to be broken. There is such beauty in brokenness. The outer shell has broken, and you get to enjoy Portia the way God intended!

In the spirit of our generation of keeping it real, please remove any cosmetics and allow my words to reveal the authenticity of who you are. The real you. The one who is really delivered and really set free and really enjoying life in Christ. She exists. The journey to her just doesn't always look like what we think. Christ has to be our model. In Mark 8:34-37 in the Message (MSG) bible it reads,

34-37 Calling the crowd to join his disciples, he said, "Anyone who intends to come with me has to let me lead. You're not in the driver's seat; I am. Don't run from suffering; embrace it. Follow me and I'll show you how. Self-help is no help at all. Self-sacrifice is the way, my way, to saving yourself, your true self. What good would it do to get everything you want and lose you, the real you? What could you ever trade your soul for?"

Don't lose the real you perpetrating as the old you. That's not cute.

Many who know me know that this book is my recurring message. No matter what I preach, when I preach to women you will hear "I'm Not That Woman." It is not necessarily a series or a message but a declaration that I echo often. My greatest desire is that you will take what you read and apply it to your life. I look forward to our discoveries together. Hit me up from time to time and let me know how you are enjoying it. Share it with your friends and especially those women who are still in discovery of who they really are. I love you guys. Happy reading!

~Portia

INTRODUCTION

Albert Einstein, one of the most famous, iconic, influential and universally admired persons in human history, was arguably one of the greatest geniuses who walked this earth. Peeping into his life's story, I am impressed with how he thought. He once said, "I have gained all earthly knowledge. I want to know how God created this world. I am not interested in this or that phenomenon, in the spectrum of this or that element, I want to know *His thoughts*." Well, me too, Albert. What are God's thoughts? What's in His mind, especially when it comes to me? How does He feel?

At an early age I had an *aha* moment. While it was a moment, this extraordinary turn of events in my life felt like decades. It was immediately after what I thought was the most embarrassing, knife-like piercing, throat gulping, public break up any young woman who swore she was in love could ever go through. While it felt like the end of my world, somehow it also felt like the most liberating, self-discovering moment. I needed to slam the door on every insecurity and self-defeating voice that tried to cripple and even paralyze me. See, in my world I was in this relationship that every person in my circle wanted. We had found young love. Girl, something real. Like... you couldn't tell me it wasn't real.

It lasted longer than the average school fling. Three out of the four years to be exact. Summers included, y'all know that's serious. We had vowed celibacy. While he was not as dedicated to his walk with God as I was, he understood my position on sex and respected it and even admired it and often told me he was glad we had made this decision. I was Boss. Like for real. Dating an athlete who I just knew *loved* me. We took professional pictures together. I wore his jersey to every game (Well, except for the one game where he had to let a cheerleader wear his number. That didn't last through the first cheer). Our connection was unique. Our relationship was admirable. I know what you are thinking, girls: You were young. But for me it was *life*. A great life. I had an awesome circle of friends. I was dedicated to my church's youth ministry. I loved life. Self-esteem was a 10. But in one day it all crumbled. In one day I had to redefine foundational truths, like successful relationships and what a strong young lady was—here is how it happened.

On this day I was confronted by a younger girl who told me she was pregnant with my boyfriend's baby. As she was telling me, her belly was literally rubbing against mine. She was *real* pregnant. As I was still processing that, hours later I learned through a family member that my boyfriend had another girlfriend who went to another school. The other girl decided to call me that evening to confirm their findings. She was real sweet and apologetic, swearing she did not know about me.

We pulled the whole "three way, you be quiet" on him. We called him, and I should have known by his tone when he answered the phone that he already knew he was being set up. I asked him about her. Knowing she was on the phone, he decided to tell me he was with her and asked why I was acting like we were still together. My mouth dropped and so did the phone. He chose her. That was the last time I ever talked to him, ever. I think the most heart-wrenching moment of all was when in the same day I learned that he was sleeping with a friend in my BFF circle as well. That probably hurt more than anything.

There I sat with a pool of emotions I could not contain. My view of myself changed. I suddenly thought, *What is wrong with me?* Every negative thought imaginable flooded my mind. Oh, and the calls, the calls didn't help. Calls of "I'm sorry, girl, I knew he was a dog" and "Girl, you didn't know? How you didn't know?" I questioned loyalty and friendship. I mean my crew, my girls? I questioned God. God, how could this happen to me. Somehow, by the grace of God I knew to turn to Him. I knew this devastating moment could change the trajectory of my life, yet the question still lingered, how was I going to go back to school? Everyone knew.

I had many options that day. And every last one of them I played out in my imagination. But it was the first time I heard, *You Are Not That Woman*. My eyes were opened. I was *woke*. I didn't just focus on myself but women in general. We all come to the fork in the road, the valley of decision. Will we let this situation define our very existence? Will I side-eye every female that gets close to me, thinking she is just the trick that wants my man? Or will I let this teach me? Can this be a situation that I can draw from the well with? I am more than how this relationship defines me. I am loved. I belong. I am rare, truly a diamond in the rough. I am a leader, an example for all women.

What was my take-away? I am *not* the woman who will cause an unnecessary scene for a boy or a friend who has yet to discover why they are breathing. I am *not* the woman who will define herself by someone else's loss. I am *not* a woman without a future, without hope, who always speaks from a self-defeating place. I am *not* a woman who finds my identity in a broken culture. *And* I sure ain't the loudmouth black chick who will turn this suburban school upside down out of rage, hurt and anger, slashing tires, bustin' windows and dismantling weaves (You can tell I thought about it... but just for a moment). I'm Not That Woman. It is something that He has told me throughout my life. I cannot say this was my last heartache or challenge with my identity, but it did start me on my road of discovery. It was the first time I truly sat and listened to God tell me what He thought of me.

Let's listen in on this conversation with God:

I think about you all the time. I even talk to you when I know you are not listening. I remember the first time we met. I took notice of everything about you. Your eyes, the crease in your forehead, the way you stare into space when you are thinking. I never look away. You are perfect. While you had the perfect shape, I noticed your heart first. How genuine you are. Pure. When I look into your eyes, I see a complete woman, not a piece, not a side piece, a hand-me-down, an afterthought, not a part—I see the whole you.

Understand, I made man, but I built woman. It took some time because I did not leave out one detail. Waiting on you seemed like an eternity. If only you could see what I see. But your lens is focused on your flaws, the things in your past, and the desired future that seems unattainable. You have this repetitive conversation beginning with "Please can you..." or "If you could only..." when I already have. When we are together, you constantly apologize for your shortcomings. It's funny, yet odd— I have known you all your life and cannot recall those things.

21

You weep from time to time and I am glad to wipe your tears. I am touched with what touches you. But I honestly wish you could feel my touch. You are so layered when you are with me. Spanx. Shapewear. Push-ups. Padding. Concealer and foundation. I am attempting to touch your soul, but sadly you think I have to go through your body. That's backwards. You believe you are shaped in iniquity. That shape is history. It dissolved when you met me.

The entire time you are talking I am touching you, but you never acknowledge my touch. You are distracted by what you call your insecurities and your inabilities. I am not sure you realize how much you talk about who and what you are not. What you don't like and how you wish you were. You repeatedly say how you were born like this, and I continually say, "You Are Born Again!" When we met you were regened. Your DNA changed. Your former life does not exist. I gave up so much to make sure your past passed away. But you believe the lie. The lies that he (Satan, Lucifer, the devil, Tyrone, John and the like), who is less than a man tells you. He is waiting for opportunities to destroy you and you give them to him. You carry my name, but I see he has touched you and you acknowledge his touch.

You keep unnecessary distance between us. I can tell you are unfamiliar with the environment I provide. It's safe, secure. It's an environment where you can rest from your work and just surrender. Allow me to handle everything. I know that scares you—you have trust issues. You are tempted to live in an environment that is not interested in seeing who you really are. I noticed that when you are in that environment you allow yourself to play a role you were not cast as. You even let them call you other names that *you answer to: fat, ugly, failure, confused, etc. That environment is toxic, but for some reason you have identified with it.*

You talk a lot. I do enjoy listening to you talk. Your conversations often remind me of others I'm still pursuing. They have a horrible habit of repeating what that fallen angel has suggested. Somehow his voice became louder than my own. It has more influence. A voice that wrongfully accuses and causes shame. Not you too. You are of me, in me. You carry my name. That name cost me something. If you could just listen to me and turn all your attention to what I am saying. Lean forward. I love intimacy and I don't rush, shout, or blame. Come closer, be quiet, and empty your mind of the lies, so I can gently whisper in your ear the truth.

You're not that woman!

~God

My conversations with God were so life altering I could not and still cannot keep them to myself. His love has to be shared. I learned that my encounters and awareness of Him caused me to forgive. I learned that He is the forgiver in me. I learned that forgiveness is powerful, and it first affects me and can certainly change the lives of others around me.

While that situation mentioned seemed so damaging to young Portia's soul, God's ability to reach me in that moment caused me to reach others who could have been otherwise lost and drowning in guilt. Like the pregnant girl. I reached out to her. I let her know that she is not alone. I became a friend to her. I even helped her find daycare for the baby. I am a woman who has the heart of God. I am a carrier of His presence. He wanted to help her and love her. He wanted her to meet Him and she did. I introduced her. Imagine that.

The *other* woman. She was to have a life-changing experience as well. She stayed with my ex-boyfriend but continued to reach out to me because somehow, she was drawn to me. I took her on as a little sister and worked with her on her self-esteem and what it really meant to be empowered by choice. Speaking to the potential she had. I became a mentor to her. She eventually dropped that dude and focused on the more important things in life—giving her life to Jesus and helping other young women. That is what God meant in Genesis by being fruitful, multiplying and re-plenishing the earth. Affecting someone's life in such a way that they have to go and do the same.

And last... my BFF in my circle. This wasn't easy at all. She shattered the girl code. Loyalty has always been big for me and this type of betrayal in my mind deserved a beating in the back ally or at minimum a hanging from the balcony moment like Morris Chestnut did to Taye Diggs for sleeping with his girl in the movie *Best Man*. But if I am being honest, I wanted her to be an outcast. I wanted her to be on the outside of our circle for what she did. I wanted all my girls to take on my feelings and treat her like the plague. That would really hurt. Because broken friendships sting like no other and I wanted her to feel that every time she saw us. But I fought that feeling and emotion. I wrestled with God on it. I asked Him to help me forgive her and to give me His eyes and His heart for her. You would not believe when surrendering to God like that how your heart can change in a moment's time. Mine did. He showed me her future.

Who she was. Both she and I were so much bigger than this moment, this dude, this school. I knew this could steal her voice and my influence. I went to her with my girls and forgave her. We were both empowered and now bigger than life itself.

Reflections

What could you be forfeiting by harboring unforgiveness in your heart towards someone?

_____

_____

_____

_____

_____

What event took place in your life that could have been for your destruction but worked out for your good?

_____

_____

_____

_____

What *I Am* statements do you need to declare daily over your life?

_____

_____

_____

_____

_____

_____

In what areas of your life do you need to reclaim your power?

_____

_____

_____

_____

_____

_____

Chapter One
LET'S GO BACK TO EDEN!

"Wrong information is not always the tool that deceives women, it's engaging in the wrong conversation."

So ladies, how did we become *that* woman in the first place? In order to discover that, we have to talk to Eve. She is my friend in my head. I have read Genesis Chapter 3 over and over again, wanting to know what really happened in that Garden. One thing I know for sure, God has a special love for women. I mean c'mon, ladies, He made man by just picking up some dirt (no shade), but He *built* a woman. He took time to make us. He put a man to sleep and carefully designed us to be the carriers in this earth. He made us *woman*, a man with a womb. What we carry internally was meant to affect our surroundings. Women have a profound presence in the atmosphere around them. You know this to be true. If mama ain't happy, then the entire house feels it. Let's explore why.

My girl Eve.

She was the real first lady. I often hear other women talk about her in a negative light: "It's Eve's fault that *Aunt Flow* comes every month." "It's her fault we have pain in childbirth." "If it wasn't for her, we could walk around all day free in our birthday suits!" "Eve messed it up for us." It's funny how we are always the judge and jury. I have learned that there are typically three sides to a story. I am sure Eve has a side. What is it? Listen in on our conversation:

Eve: *You know, Portia, just like most women, I too admire beautiful things. Sure, I heard what God said, but there was another voice in that Garden. Portia, there is always another voice!*

The interesting thing about deception is you don't know you are being deceived. I was placed in this perfect place with nothing and no one to compare myself to. No Real Housewives, no Cookie Lyons, no thirsty chick who stole my man's attention. None of that. Before plastic surgery and butt injections, I was perfect, but somehow my eyes were opened to imperfections. When I saw that beautiful creature fly out of the east side of Eden, I thought, Wow what is that? Who is that? This has to be from God! Maybe this is God? I want to touch him; I want to talk to him. Look at his wings! Look at his colors! I would have never guessed he was an enemy to my destiny.

What I know now is that Satan takes on many different shapes, forms and characteristics to deceive women. I hear many women ask, "Why was she talking to a snake?" Girl, tell them he wasn't a snake—yet. Women talk and spend time with snakes every day and don't even know it. But now I realize they only entertain these deadly conversations because they are not as familiar with the voice, the voice that will help them recognize the counterfeit. And not just recognize it, but not even desire to listen to it. That voice that is so affirming, so liberating. It will lead them into the destiny that He pre-arranged for them. His voice that says they are authentically beautiful and they need no addi-

tions or alterations.

That snake likes to be the man in every woman's life. His motive is to be the voice that is loudest. Think about it: Why do you think he came for me and not Adam? Think about how God made us. Think about our anatomy. Women were created open. We were created to receive, to carry, and finally to birth. We are carriers. I mean, just think about it. It's not hard for women to get things done. Just say the word and we are carrying it out. We are adaptable, flexible, suitable for any and every situation. It's how we were made. But nothing is carried out unless a seed is first planted. Babies are not born without the seed of a man. Everything starts with a seed. Portia, words are seed. But we as women have a choice whether or not to receive it.

Portia: *Wait, pause... I am a bit confused. So Eve, if you had a choice, why did you choose to receive what he said?*

Eve: [*Poking out her lips and rolling her eyes*] *Girl, the same reason why women receive and carry out what that snake is still saying today—He mixes the truth with lies. He's accessing their souls. There is so much to that, but we can continue that conversation later. Let me leave you with this: Through our Father's redemption plan, He has restored women. And though the snake is still running his mouth, through my story you now know you don't have to receive anything he says. The key is becoming intimate with the Father's voice so when that snake approaches, you can simply look down and let him know, "Don't come for me because I did not send for you—I'm Not That Woman."*

~Eve

The first question we have to ask ourselves, ladies, is why did the serpent approach the woman and not the man. I mean if he really wanted to wreck mankind, why not approach the man who God gave the specific instructions to? Why go for the woman? What was so attractive about Eve that the serpent was drawn to and what was it about him that caused her to lose her focus? I guess we can ask ourselves this today in real time. Who or what is the cause behind us losing our focus and why are we so drawn to people and things that distract us from our purpose? Why don't we finish things? Why do we become so frustrated with outside circumstances, knowing that the real change has to start on the inside? How did we become the woman who complains about everything? Or the woman who never seems to be satisfied? Always left wanting more?

Just like Eve, living in paradise, got a man that loves her and has a job but is still looking for something else. Where does this emptiness come from? Why are you still coming for me, serpent? What do I have that you want? It's simple—*access*.

Women are the door. We are receivers. God made us that way. Look at the anatomy of a female. We were created open. Our sexual organ is created open, where a man's is closed. Our design has purpose and the enemy knew it.

The enemy *knows* it. He approached the woman to gain access to her soul. To sow his vision as seed on the inside of her for her to carry out. He knew if he could say the right words, sown in deception, she would receive them and carry them out.

Married ladies, think about this for just a second: After sex, men typically fall asleep. I mean you may get a little after sex affection for a few brownie points, but for the most part your husband is drained, tired. He released something, and strength left him. Ironically you may have been exhausted before sex, but afterwards, you got a lot going on mentally. You are thinking. Sometimes to the point you have to get up and do something. Maybe think and clean the entire house at midnight. All of a sudden you've got the missing link to starting the family empire and you get up to write a business plan, or you just have this unsolicited energy that keeps you up. *Why?* Because you are a receiver. You just received through your sexual relationship all that was in that man's soul and the two became one.

It's actually brilliant. A relationship is about the exchange of strengths and weaknesses. We typically tend to get with guys who are our opposite. Through our sexual relationships we become one physically, emotionally and spiritually. We make an exchange. He is a visionary. He plugs in and releases everything he's got into us and we typically get up, knowing how to carry it out.

You know how men can be, they can talk a good game. They can talk about vision and what they want to do all day long. But what are we thinking most of the time? Well... *Let's do it*. Most times he just doesn't know how. That's where you come in. You know how to put feet to the vision. You just needed the seed. You just needed him to plug in. You just needed to receive. I speak to a lot of married ladies who seem to complain about not being on the same page with their spouse. They say things like, "I just don't get him" or "I don't see what he's saying." Sometimes my answer is, "When's the last time you gave him some?"

or "Girl, how often are you giving him some?" Get in the bed and continue that process of becoming one. Let him plug in, in ways he hasn't before, and I promise you, you will get it!

But here is the thing. This brilliant thing called sex works whether you are married or not, *single ladies*. You become one during that time whether you are married or not. It can be absolutely dangerous and detrimental to your life both physically and emotionally. It's like what the late Dr. Myles Monroe said, "If you don't know the purpose of a thing, abuse is inevitable." That especially holds true for sex. Every man you sleep with is releasing something and gaining access to your soul. It's the reason why we tend to be confused as women sometimes about what direction we need to go in life. It's because Anthony had one vision and then Caleb had another and finally James has another, and we slept with all of them. That is too many visions. It creates division and now we have an internal conflict in the area of our souls.

It is why in Proverbs Chapter 31:1-3 (ESV), King Lemuel gives us such a poetic recap of the words of his mother.

The words of King Lemuel. An oracle that his mother taught him:

2 What are you doing, my son?[a] What are you doing, son of my womb?

What are you doing, son of my vows?

3 Do not give your strength to women, your ways to those who destroy kings.

33

One thing I tell my spiritual sons is don't give your strength to women. The wrong women. The Proverbs Chapters 6 and 7 women. Don't release in places that are going to drain you. You wonder why your son has no vision, can't keep a career, never knows what to do. It's because he has given away his strength through his seed. No wonder he still lives with you. Tell him to stop sleeping around. He has released his vision and it's destroying his ability to rule as a king and to judge justly.

You get it yet? I want to lean in a little further. I want you to truly understand how this serpent gets us repeatedly. I promise you, Eve is celebrating in paradise knowing that you are reading this. It reminds me of the scene in the movie *Independence Day* when Will Smith and Jeff Goldblum took the enemy mothership down and had to communicate to the militias around the country the strategies to overcoming the enemy. Well here you go.

The enemy had to gain access to Eve's soul. Your soul is made up of your mind, your will, and your emotions. It has many functions. It is what makes up your personality. Much like the role of the Holy Spirit in the trinity—it leads and guides you, it's your intellect. The soul is generally regarded as that part of you that holds the life principle. Though it is not visible, it is attached to and a part of your physical body. The soul is the *seat of your emotions*, your will and your moral actions. It is where you feel, and you know as women we know how to feel. Your soul is the area where you think and make your decisions.

Your soul can be fragmented like pieces of a pie. You can allow people or things to attach to a part of your soul and sometimes you cannot move forward and experience total freedom because your soul is tied to things that are ungodly and end up giving you negative outcomes. You can literally give pieces of your soul away. *Literally*. Feeling incomplete? This is your answer.

A soul tie is an emotional connection or a bond to another that unites you. The bible explores soul ties first in the way God intended. Sometimes you have to go back to the maker to get the original intent of a thing. The bible uses words like knit or cleave or bind, which means to bring close together, follow close after, be attached to someone, or adhere to one another as glue. We first see the use of these words in Genesis with the first couple.

Therefore shall a man leave his father and his mother and shall cleave unto his wife: and they shall be one flesh (Genesis 2:24).

Many times you cannot give your entire self to God because part of your soul is knit or tied to someone else. So while you are endeavoring to have this awesome worship experience, something is missing. It's because you were made to pour out your soul to Him and worship Him in spirit and in truth. My girl Hannah is a great example of that in 1 Samuel. She was bitter because of her infertility and was so blinded by not being able to produce a baby that she couldn't see anything else, not even her husband. Her soul was tied up in bitterness. The bible said that she went to church and poured out her soul before the Lord. To the point that the Pastor thought she was drunk (I bet you ain't NEVA cried out to God like that). She had to let go of those bitter and negative emotions and call her soul back from that wasted place. She had to stop rocking her inability to conceive like a baby and allowing that to become her identity. I believe in her time of pouring out she was saying, "I'M NOT THAT INFERTILE WOMAN! I give that over to you LORD. I am looking beyond my pain and seeing the promise. I am calling my soul back from this. I am whole in my soul".

Maybe you never feel fully knitted together with your spouse. Could it be a fragment of your emotions is still with an old relationship? You are still united with him? He still has a piece of you, so when your lips said, "I do," your soul said, "I can't because I'm not all here." You have repeat patterns of depression, oppression, feelings of loneliness even when in relationships. God wants these patterns broken.

The bible says in 1 Thessalonians 5:23-24 (Message),

May God Himself, the God who makes everything holy and whole, make you holy and whole, put you together—Spirit, soul, and body—and keep you fit for the coming of our Master, Jesus Christ. The One who called you is completely dependable. If He said it, He'll do it!

I love that. It says May God Himself. Meaning He will take care of this situation. Only God knows how you are tied and how to untie you. God knows where you left a piece of your soul. Why did Jesus come in the first place? To set the captives *free!* To destroy the work of the enemy, to let you know you don't have to be that woman anymore. God wants you to be whole in your soul. The bible says in Psalm 23 that He can restore your soul. Bring it back together again. What you need to do is partner with God and call your soul back from every wasted place. Every wasted relationship. Call your soul back from abuse and addiction. From extramarital affairs. Call your soul back from abortions and abandonment. Call your soul back from emotional affairs and impurity.

The bible says in Ephesians 4:27 [Amplified Bible (AMP)],

Leave no such room or foothold for the devil [give no opportunity to him].

This means you no longer allow the enemy to gain access to your soul. Don't allow him to gain access to how you think, how you feel or how you make decisions. Don't allow him to plug in. Let him know I'm *occupied*. There is no room here for you.

In Genesis Chapter 3 he approached Eve to gain access to her soul, so it could affect the way she thought, the way she felt, and it ultimately led to the decision of high treason in the garden. He released seed. Word seeds and she received them. She carried it out.

What did the first couple do once they were exposed? They hid themselves. Sound familiar? Haven't you done that? Tried to cover up something in your soul that you didn't want anyone to see? The thought of being vulnerable to anyone makes you sick. You now have to wear a mask of protection in fear that the exposure will cause rejection. They were naked! But my question to you is who are you naked? Who are you without all the layers of insecurities disguised in success and titles? Who are you without the make-up and the lashes? Who are you when you are not the one giving the advice or being strong for others? Who are you in the garden? Who are you without the clothes? Who are you really if we take your assignments in life away, mother, wife... Who are you naked?

Eve's Review

- Don't give your attention to things that distract you from your purpose.

- Don't cover up your feelings and wrong belief system with a religiously correct fig leaf like I did.

- God desires truth in your inward parts (Psalms 51:6).

- Deception comes out of insecurity. It was not until I had an experience with the enemy that I became insecure and hid myself.

- Women are moved by what we hear. I heard what he said, received it and carried it out. What are you hearing?

- A controlling woman will always produce a passive man.

- God cannot lie. The enemy mixes lies with the truth.

- Honesty in the dictionary is defined as freedom from deceit and fraud.

Reflections

Write down the lies you have believed about yourself and replace them with the truth of God's Word.

_____

_____

_____

_____

_____

_____

What patterns do you follow that cause you to lose your focus?

_____

_____

_____

_____

_____

What have you covered up that needs to be exposed for healing?

_____

_____

_____

_____

_____

_____

_____

Chapter Two
COVER GIRL

Let's Get Naked

I am naked without anything on.

Stripped of everything that I allowed to define me.

No more layers to hide me, no comparisons to camouflage me.

Who Am I Naked?

Naked, I am His choice. I am God's glory. Look at me, what do you see?

It doesn't matter because I see me, who I was created to be,

Without all the unnecessary accessories or you telling me what to be.

I am so free to be me. No fig trees or leaves to hide me.

Naked with scars or imperfections no longer equals insecurities.

I am flawless because He sees me. I see me.

Naked is the real Me.

~P

I recently ran across a Cover Girl ad that said, "I Am What I Make Up" as a tag line. Sometimes I think we really believe that. While I appreciate make-up and all that we can put on to cover up, there is nothing more beautiful than naked, bare, pure and real. Think about it. We love Jesus because of His scars. They tell the story of our redemption.

Left uncovered we are vulnerable. Yes, I said what is a curse word to many of us. *Vulnerable*. Nothing, at least in our eyes, protecting us from the criticism, judgment and even uncertainties that come with showing ourselves without anything "extra."

There are times I step out of the traditional format in my speaking engagements and do a "Girl, Let Me Tell You" segment. It is a time I choose to be vulnerable. To show my scars, proving there is beauty in ashes and share some lessons learned through life as a woman. In these segments, I often ask the question, "Who are you naked?" I promise you each time I ask, women look back at me with the side-eye. Why? Because we have been tricked into thinking naked is bad. It isn't a good word. Naked is how we came into this world and honestly, how we will go out.

Sometimes I don't think we realize how much we really conform to this world. We allow this world to tell us what we like and don't like. How to talk and walk and how to dress. What to do and not to do. But if you are stripped of everything the world has put on you, who are you in your purest most vulnerable state? What do you like? What would you really be doing with your life? Would you be as guarded if you were stripped of your experiences? Your victories and defeats? If I took your titles and assignments in life from you, would you have purpose? If I burned everything you think you need to put on to look better, appear "put-together," could you look in the mirror naked and actually like what you see? Selah.

I can tell you today that I love myself naked. But that was not always the case. For me, comparing myself to others early in life is what nearly crippled me. I remember the day I had to actually take the time to prove I was even female. Go with me back to 1985.

"But, I *am* a girl!"

For years it was difficult for me to forget that I actually had to utter those words out of my mouth. I was eight years old and my mom had to cut my hair all the way down into a small fro because a neighborhood kid had cut my hair. I hated it. When she cut it, I could barely look in the mirror, but she and my aunt assured me I had such a pretty face and that I was more than my hair. That gave me the ounce of confidence I needed to show up to school the next day. It was a normal day, and everything was fine until lunch. That day, our lunch aide was a substitute, one we never had. She asked all the boys and girls to separate into two lines as she was releasing the girls first for recess. As I was leaving out the door, laughing with my friends, she grabbed me by my arm and said,

"Get in *your* line. What are you trying to pull? I said girls first!"

"But, I *am* a girl," I told her with a shaky voice and tears that welled up in my eyes.

The girls gasped, the boys laughed, and soon enough the entire cafeteria was staring at me. Embarrassed, the aide apologized, but that apology could not correct the damage to my soul.

For the first time while at recess I began to take notice of the other girls' hair. I was the minority amongst many Caucasians. Most of them with flowy blonde hair and even most of the black girls in my school had beautifully permed hair with bouncy curls. *Not me*, I noticed. *Why can't I look like them? Everybody probably thinks I look like a boy.* This was my first memory of feeling inadequate, insecure and comparing myself to others.

Appearance is one of the first and easiest comparisons we make in life. From the professionally styled and overly photoshopped celebrities in the media, to your impeccable friend who telecommutes and has no kids. She can spend hours in the gym while you can barely make it twice a week. You work a 9-5 and have two children, three if you count the dog. So we "body shame" ourselves and once in a while feel good about our appearance when we run across someone we think we look better than. Or better yet, let's talk about performance comparison. This also can start in school. From who is better than who at what, to who received the award and who didn't, to who gets the better grades in your household. It all graduates and transfers into adulthood onto our jobs, the titles, what we accomplish in life and we end up miserable.

What is it about humanity that always has to see someone else when they see you? The entire basketball season you hear nothing but comparisons. Is LeBron James better than Michael Jordan? How does Stephen Curry's game compare to LeBron's? Oh, he reminds me of such 'n' such in his day. Why can't we be individuals? Truth is we are. We are too unique to be compared fairly. While someone's "game" may remind you of another's, truth is, it's never going to be the same.

We have a natural tendency to make comparisons as a system of developing logic and reasoning. Somehow our comparisons give us value in our lives. I don't believe the answer is to stop the comparing, but to change who we are comparing ourselves to. I think we have to compare ourselves to ourselves. Measure yourself against yourself. Simply put, be the best you, that you were created to be.

My trainer said something to me that totally changed my life. I was telling him I would be missing some days of training the following week due to a conference I had to speak at. He asked what I was speaking on. I told him I was not sure. I speak at this conference every year and I was one of the last speakers of the conference and sometimes that leaves you with nothing to say. Everybody has said everything. He looked at me and said, "There is never any new content. Everything that is ever going to be said has been said. Just listen to only what you said last year and make a point to say it better. You are better this year, so say it better." He was telling me to only compare myself to myself. *It worked!*

The bible says in Galatians 6:4 (MSG),

Make a careful exploration of who you are and the work you have been given, and then sink yourself into that. Don't be impressed with yourself. Don't compare yourself with others. Each of you must take responsibility for doing the creative best you can with your own life.

I learned how to take responsibility for doing the creative best with my own life by being a better me and not comparing myself to others. Truth is, no one can be me. No one can look exactly like I look, produces how I produce. Only I can do that. I encourage you to do and be what only you can do and be. Listen to yourself and say it better next time. Watch yourself and do it better next time. Don't rob us or this world because you are too busy comparing yourself to others and getting stuck because most times it's just incomparable.

And please, don't allow the lunch aide to challenge your version of beauty. Beauty is in the eye of the beholder and recognize you only have to look in the mirror.

It's why Adam and Eve hid themselves in the garden. After their encounter with the enemy, they saw how the world would see them and came up with "that's bad." It took them out of position with God and their affirmation of who they were. Today I say to you, come out of hiding and when you do come out, come out *naked*. Don't put on a fabricated personality to keep from being rejected. Don't put on sarcasm because you are afraid to articulate how you really feel. And puleeeese don't put on that fake ole fur called a security blanket you have been wearing around, thinking it is protecting you from being hurt. You have been wearing it so long it stinks, and you can't even smell it. It smells like a wet dog because you are sweating fake identity.

I promise you, naked is better. Being naked helps you to make choices from an authentic place. It even helps you to see through the façades others try to give you and love them for who they are. It deepens and strengthens your relationships because they are rooted in truth not lies. We say things like "they ain't ready for me," but reveal yourself bare, don't wait for them to be "ready." We were not made to have alter egos or split personalities based on our environments or social settings.

Personally, when I began to take off all the "clothes" this world gave me and was stripped of everything I allowed to define me (it's the pruning process), I liked me. I never hated myself, but I did second guess myself. I did define beautiful incorrectly. I defined success by what this world showed me instead of living in my purpose.

I thank God for being stripped. I found out what I really like. Simple things like honesty. Just tell me what you think, and I will do the same and we will go from there. I love to give people compliments instead of comparing myself to them. I now see the beauty in everyone. Yes, even the friend who runs her mouth and gets on our nerves. She is actually cool. I allow her to be safe naked and we have a good time. Naked—I actually like my bare legs. They are strong and shaped well. Naked—I like my face. I don't need to try to cover it up anymore. It's really cute. So, what do you like? Let's identify and abandon those things and live in our *real truth*, our nakedness.

"Everybody is a genius, but if you judge a fish by its ability to climb a tree, it will live its whole life believing it is stupid."

~Albert Einstein

Reflections

Who do you compare yourself to and why?

_____

_____

_____

_____

_____

Who are you *naked*? What do you need to strip yourself of?

_____

_____

_____

_____

What does vulnerability mean to you?

_____

_____

_____

_____

_____

List things that you like about yourself (character, physical and personality).

_____

_____

_____

_____

_____

_____

Chapter Three

MY GIRRRRRLFRIEND

One of my all-time favorite TV sitcoms was *Girlfriends* with my girls Joan, Maya, Lynn and Toni. It was a show released in 2000 focusing on a diverse group of black women who walked through life's tests, trials and triumphs together. Everything from babies, to dating, marriage, divorce, promotions, homelessness and entrepreneurship. They supported one another through it all. For me it was a great comedic, yet honest display of true friendship. But at the end of the day it was a show. It was still just a display of what the writer wanted you to see. In real life I have seen friendships among women play out very differently. I could not write this book without addressing it because I believe it is essential to the emotional, spiritual and psychological development of every woman. I often find myself saying to women in counseling, "Girl, you need a real friend!"

When we live uncovered, I believe we can have more fulfilling relationships with each other. Especially women. There is nothing like strong friendships among women. I think every woman needs other women. But the enemy has also played us against each other. You really have to understand the gates of life. Things get into our hearts through our eyes and our ears. Proverbs 4:20-27 [New International Version(NIV)] tells us,

My son, pay attention to what I say; turn your ear to my words. Do not let them out of your sight, keep them within your heart; for they are life to those who find them and health to one's whole body. Above all else, guard your heart, for everything you do flows from it. Keep your mouth free from perversity; keep corrupt talk far from your lips. Let your eyes look straight ahead fix your gaze directly before you. Give careful thought to the paths for your feet and be steadfast in all your ways. Do not turn to the right or the left; keep your foot from evil.

What that boils down to is we are what we let in. We have given too much of our attention to how this world defines relationship and not God.

Reality television has dominated our society. This genre is so appealing because it aims to present real people in their everyday lives. People who they think we can identify with. It has made us utter the words, *"Girl, that's me!" (Really? As petty as she is?)* You Are Not Her! A recurring theme I have noticed is "girl hate." Women pulling each other's weaves out over men. "Mean Girls" rallying a posse to exclude someone. And these aren't adolescents, they are *grown tail* women who never dealt with their insecurities and need for acceptance from the wrong sources. I have a saying, "High school never ends." Funny thing is, I loved high school. I still have genuine, meaningful relationships from high school. (Shout out to my Seneca Valley Crew.) But those were the days when the word *girl* was at its peak.

See, *girl* is defined as an immature female. We just

needed to grow up, but for many of us it just didn't happen. Just because we got older doesn't mean we matured. We still are the little girl who takes a sneak peek at Lisa's body and twist her mouth and say, "She *ain't* all that." But who am I kidding; this theme didn't start with reality television. The seed was planted in the Garden of Eden when Satan got Eve to see herself differently than how God saw her. She had nothing to compare herself to and now all of a sudden, she sees what she is not.

We compare ourselves amongst ourselves and that is breeding ground for unnecessary division amongst women. The bigger issue is with self. We were all born with four basic needs: acceptance, security, identity, and purpose. When those needs are not fulfilled, we settle for the counterfeits that cause us to be inauthentic. God created us with those needs and the plan was always to get them filled from Him. But don't get it twisted, God uses people. The connection that women have when we truly come together is priceless. Once we realize the true value of friendship amongst women and what we gain and have the opportunity to impart, we can end the propaganda and "keep some hair!"

I want to let you in on a conversation with Leah. She can be found in Genesis 29. She can really talk to us about a missed opportunity to have a God-ordained relationship, the one with her sister. She was given in marriage by trickery of her father to a man named Jacob who didn't love her. Jacob eventually married her sister, Rachel, who he really loved, and "girl hate" was alive once again!

Leah: *As I stand here at my sister's grave I realize that I never really knew her. I can tell you what she looked like because I always compared myself to her. She was beauti-*

52

ful. I can tell you every piece of clothing she had. I can talk to you about her flawless skin and perfect shape. I can tell you that, but I never told her. I never told her I thought she was beautiful. I never told her much of anything good about herself. She had the love of our husband, something I didn't have but wanted. I had his children, something she didn't have but wanted. She was barren for so long. She wanted children so badly and because I was hurting in ways I could not explain, I used the one thing that she wanted against her. All I can rehearse in this moment are the displays of my jealousy and envy of her. Remembering how Jacob looked at her. My eyes are swelling with tears. It's regret. I cannot tell you much about her, like her favorite color, her secret thoughts that only sisters share. How she felt when she finally had my nephew, Joseph. I never prayed with her in her painful moments. I never even hugged her. I cannot tell you what made her laugh. I cannot tell you the normal things sisters share. I wasted time hating her—all over a man. She is gone now.

Rachel had problems conceiving. I never even asked her about her infertility struggles. How it made her feel and it was that very thing that killed her. She died having her second child. I wasn't even there in that moment. I was in my tent thinking, now she is getting the best of both worlds. All I could think of was how Jacob would love her sons more than mine. I'm just the baby-mama—she's the wife. But regardless of all those circumstances, she was my sister and now I miss her. I miss the relationship we never had. I am imagining our children playing together as we have girl chats in the tent. She could have taught me some hair tips. Her's was always well put together. I could have helped her with Joseph more—he had such a smart mouth (LOL). I am only imagining, but it could be your reality.

~Leah

Leah teaches us to not be the woman who lives in regret because she did not allow herself to have true connections in life. Don't be the woman who isolates herself because the little girl in her is afraid of being rejected. Be the woman who reaches out first. Who fosters meaningful relationships with other women. Who gives of herself even when it's inconvenient. Most of all be the woman who drowns in the realities of God's love for her. It is from that place we can overcome any obstacle and have lasting relationships.

Leah eventually realized that her life was not simply defined by her ability to have children and feel unloved. She realized how much God loved her through the gift of her sons. God wiped away the tears of rejection, a touch no man can compare to. Leah found true love. The love of a Father— He filled in the gaps!

Sociologist Janet Lever states the difference between girls' relationships and boys' relationships. Girls tend to feel more comfortable with a single best friend where boys prefer to play on teams. Girls tend to have an open show of affection with their girlfriends, both physically and verbally while boys are less intimate. I believe it just speaks to how we were made as women. We will nurture the mess out of anything! Even those of us who are less "touchy feely" people, we still know how to provide the care that another person needs. This is why most women don't do well when an intimate relationship between friends ends. Studies show women need connection; men need status.

While it's cool to have guys for friends, many women who only have guy friends do so because they have been so deeply hurt or betrayed by members of their own sex, they no longer pursue friendships with them. Don't be that woman. You are missing out on something unique when you don't lend yourself to true relationships between women. I am not just talking about when you are a child or a teenager or even during your college years but even as adults. You can have authentic, deep meaningful relationships with women—yes, women! These friendships bring out the selflessness in all of us. They demand vulnerability and time, two ingredients we all so often want to leave out. But they give back in unimaginable ways. I thought about this through a pretty funny experience I had. Relationships reveal who you are. But if you are not vulnerable or open to feedback you could be caught with all your stuff hanging out and don't even know. Listen to what happened to me.

It was the summer of 2001. It was a very busy time in my life where my career was concerned because as a government contracted meeting planner, I was traveling all over the country. This particular week, I happened to be grounded and was doing half-days in the office. Excited to get home early and actually cook a meal for my husband and set up some kind of "at home" date night, I packed up my desk, got my keys and purse and was ready to head for the door when I realized I had to use the ladies room. I had a long ride ahead of me as I planned to take the metro home. I sat my purse and keys down, told my co-worker who I shared a corner office with to watch my stuff while I journeyed to the ladies' room. I was in a hurry and wanted to get on the metro before it became too crowded, so I did a light jog there. I walked out of the ladies' room, came back into the office and said good-bye to my co-worker. I got on the elevator that was packed with people to the lobby. When I stepped off, I said good-bye to the trusty security guy at the desk and proceeded to head across the major crowded road to the metro station. As I swiftly walked across the street, I heard a loud voice. I didn't think it was anyone talking to me so I tried to ignore it, but the voice kept getting louder. I finally gave ear to what I was hearing and turned around. There was a young lady with a scarf on her head and looked to be sucking a lollipop, like she just came from the corner store. As she popped her lips and pointed her finger I heard the words, "HEY GIRL! YOUR BOOTY HANGING OUT!"

I was wearing a cute navy dress that stopped right above the knee and somehow when I used the bathroom, moments prior, I tucked my dress in my underwear and kept it moving. Now, don't judge me, I had a lot on my mind, after all I was trying to get home for my date night. Now as she is screaming these words at me, all I could think about was the co-worker that I shared my office with that didn't say one word, or the 6 or 7 people in the elevator that my back-side was exposed to that did not bother to mention my "drawls" were out, nor did the security officer that I took the time to say bye to and turned around and walk away. Surely he saw my back-side. Newsflash people - I can't see my own butt!!!

While this story is hilarious, I will never forget the revelation I received out of it and often share with my audience – You can't see your butt. We all have blind spots in our life. It's actually good. If we had an aerial view of who we were, we would not need the relationships that God has put us in to make us better. Everyone needs people in their life that can give it to them straight, no chaser. That can lift up your shirt and show you your backside or better yet, let you know that something that should be covered is hanging out. More so you have to be able to hear it. See I heard someone trying to get my attention but I didn't really incline my ear so I could make the necessary adjustments. I even asked myself why didn't anyone close to me say anything? Were they scared of my reaction? Did they not know how to communicate my "flaw" to me?

Now ask yourself who can speak into your life? Do you only have those around you that agree with you, praise you, but never offer the constructive criticism we all need to be better? The Bible says that, "Iron sharpens Iron". Who in your life makes you sharp? Your spouse? A best friend? Even your children can be used to show you—You. And when what was once in your blind spot is brought into your plain view, make the necessary adjustments and keep it moving.

Once I got over the initial embarrassment that I showed the community my butt, I simply pulled my dress out of my underwear, giggled a little bit, thanked the urban young lady that was bold enough to scream across the street and kept it moving.

Because we have given so much attention to women's relationships that don't work, many of us have not had ones that really do. Whether it is your 20-year-long relationships (I have those☺) or the pop ups that enter your life unexpectedly but touch you in ways that are endless even after they are gone.

I appreciate programs the schools and churches offer (at least my school and church did) for self-esteem enhancement for women. It was there in my SEE and Sister 2 Sister programs, respectively, where I learned that many times we have bad relationships because we have a defeated view of our own selves. That view is rooted in the fear of what others may think of us, so we learn at a very early age how to mask up and pretend. How to only show others what we think they want to see. Our younger years often didn't correctly teach us life skills like communication. How to articulate when we are hurting and how to have good healthy confrontation in friendships. Missing out on these skills will lead us to a life of misguided expectations, assumptions and hiding in relationships.

I can't tell you the countless number of times as a young person I was called into "meetings" with either my counselor in school or my youth minister at church about friendship issues. I was usually called as a mediator because I was always the one they expected to "pull up" and be the example for my peers or I was being reprimanded for leaving someone out of my "group of friends." Those conversations usually went something like this:

Stacy feels like you guys leave her out of things on purpose. You need to make a better effort to include her in on your activities. Talk to her more. Portia (and here it comes), maybe you should spend some one-on-one time with her. In my head I would always think, Do you know why Stacy feels that way? Did you know that Stacy acts stank and standoffish? Do you realize Stacy is not a "group" friend and she is territorial and wants me all to herself? And another thing, Why can't Stacy speak for herself? But I would just listen and spend a lifetime trying to make Stacy feel like she is a part of the crew when truth is, Stacy will never be satisfied until Stacy is good with Stacy.

Honestly, I have had many Stacys in my life. As an adult (it looks a little different but same principle) and as a child. I have worked a lifetime making women feel comfortable, but in doing this I've learned a lot about them and myself. I learned you don't have to be friends with everyone, but it is in our nature, especially as Christian women, to be inclusive. You don't have to label everyone best friend or even have them in your "Fave 5." Friendship is a covenant word and that means more than just a casual acquaintance. I've learned to appreciate the different relationships I have with different women and they are all unique in nature. I've learned when you have a group of friends, just let it be what it is. Don't try to make anyone feel more or less special because the other friend is around. I also learned that when it comes to relationships, women are territorial, and it actually starts as little girls.

One thing at 40 years of age I realize is that in relationships many things point back to rejection and acceptance. As we mature and have relationships as adults this still holds true. Upon meeting someone, most women know whether this will be a friend or an acquaintance. What the relationship will be often hinges on whether we feel accepted. Most of our closest friends are people who have accepted us with all of our flaws and personality traits. My friends who truly know me know that I work hard at filters in non-intimate relationships, but with my "inner court," there is no filter. Not because I don't care about their feelings but because we have spent enough time with one another for them to know my heart. I always have their best interests at heart and I want to tell them like it is, so they get it the first time. No sugar coating, just straight. But someone who doesn't really know me and is trying to get to know me can be easily offended by my approach. They may walk away and say she is just rude and the next time they see me they are acting strange and I may view that as rejection.

Many people who have suffered at the evilness of rejection don't do friendships well. Rejection causes you to develop fabricated personalities. You become someone who you are not in order to be accepted. Rejection also produces the tendency to reject others so that you aren't the first to be rejected. "Mean girls" are developed this way. Rejection keeps you wondering if people like you. Girl, I will tell you now that is too much work. Let me tell you like grandma told me—everybody ain't going to like you. It's ok, you will find your tribe. Just be *you*. You will find some relationships are literally not good for you. They drain you. They take, take and take again. Every relationship you are in should be balanced. It should include receiving and giving. Sometimes you have to categorize your relationships. It's ok. Some people may just be mentees more than friends. You are just pouring into them for a season. If we get this mixed up, we can get easily agitated with someone who was not meant to be a friend at that time.

I have also seen rejection drive women into wanting to fit into everything. You join everything because acceptance and affirmation from others is like a drug for you. It gives you a false sense of belonging. This is so dangerous because when you don't have things, activities and titles to define you any longer, you don't know who you are, and depression can be a result of that. Women who battle with rejection tend to have overly opinionated personalities and the need to be right about most things. I know we all love those women (LOL). *We are telling them to **shut up** in our heads*. And then we see this nasty root show up in other ways in relationships. The friend who agrees with everything because she fears confrontation. She is like this because her identity is based upon what people think of her. If you have a friend like this, try to help her by asking her opinion more than you used to. Let her know it is safe to share who she is with you in the confines of your friendship. Many times women who deal with rejection have low self-esteem and wallow in self-pity. They feel badly about themselves, so they don't share themselves. I always say that insecurity is truly the ultimate insult to God. It tells God that when He made you He didn't make you good enough. You are essentially blaming God, which is demonic territory.

The bible gives us beautiful displays of relationships and true friendships. Have you ever asked yourself why Mary had to go and spend time with Elizabeth after the news that she herself was carrying Jesus, the Messiah? I have. Mary and Elizabeth had more in common than we may think. Both of their husbands' initial reactions to the supernatural conception of the children they were going to bring forth were negative. They needed each other. Friendship among women is a gift. I can imagine both had fears of what others would think about their pregnancies and not just others but their husbands. *You know they talked about it.* Elizabeth being barren most of her life would now bring forth a son in her old age. People talked about her when she was barren, and they were probably talking about her again—how in the world were she and Zachariah going to raise that child as old as they were?

Mary becoming pregnant before she was married, telling folk God did it (LOL). But somehow when they got together they understood one another. I am sure the fellowship was amazing. It was safe. It felt right. They got each other. It was something they both needed at that time in their lives, so much so Elizabeth's physical body had a reaction upon seeing Mary. Her baby leaped in her womb. She was filled with the Holy Ghost and began to prophecy. What a picture of acceptance for Mary. God knew they needed each other because each of them would later face the worst thing a mother could face. The loss of a child.

Loneliness could have knocked on both of their doors. Loneliness does not come because you are alone. Loneliness is an emotion that can come from a lack of connection. Many married women are lonely. Women with children and boyfriends and people all around them all the time still sometimes have a sense of loneliness.

Being alone can be a beneficial and enjoyable experience if it is a situation you choose to be in. Loneliness, isolation and rejection are feelings of disjointedness from others, which can be damaging. These feelings often lead to people becoming fearful of being alone. God promises to never leave us nor forsake us. He shows up in our lives, often through other people. I can testify in my deepest darkest hours when I felt alone and also wanted to be alone, not because I did not want people around but because my grief was so deep, I didn't know how to allow anyone in my space. I thank God that He uses friendships to pull you out of your pit. I saw this clearly in my conversation with Ruth. Her ability to stick with Naomi, her mother-in-law, was a great example of friendship.

Ruth: *Portia, the road ahead looked dangerous and uncertain. But I wasn't going back. Never go back. Literally the road from Moab to Judah was rumored to have men who would rob and kill women. I didn't care. I was sticking with Naomi, my mother-in-law. We were going together. I would overcome every obstacle and she would be with me. Many people's problems are magnified while in the middle of adversity. They become islands to themselves, not realizing that God has created us with the power to form deep and lasting relationships. The right relationship literally saved my life.*

See my mother-in-law, Naomi, was very bitter after the loss of her husband and sons, one of which was my husband. She wore her bitterness like a robe. She refused to hide her suffering and it turned into hopelessness. But our connection was too deep for me to abandon her. From the day I met her she told me about her God. Somehow through her I knew there was new life. She introduced me to a God I never knew and because of that, I decided I would live. Not just for me but also for her until she realized there was life still in her. Her bitterness was no match for my love and when she thought it was over, I knew that it was just the beginning. It's all about perspective. I didn't really know God like she did, but somehow, I couldn't blame Him for our tragedy. As we traveled I felt closer and closer to my harvest (a fruitful city). While together, Naomi asked me to call her Mara. It means bitter. I refused. Naomi means joy and I knew if we just kept traveling, joy would come. And it did.

Portia, don't ever stop traveling. Don't ever just do nothing. Don't park in a place that won't produce for you.

Don't allow life to just happen or wait for the "rapture" to rescue you from sorrow. Grab hold of new opportunities and when they don't come, create them like I did. I wasn't going back to Moab. For what? For who? The risk I took led to redemption. I knew that all I went through and staying with Naomi was not just coincidence, but it was orchestrated. Now we both have a life—a new life.

~Ruth

I thank God that Ruth echoed to Naomi what I have said many times in life—You Are Not That Woman!

Reflections

Who are the friends in your life that you are most vulnerable with?

_____

_____

_____

_____

_____

What do you do when you feel rejected?

_____

_____

_____

_____

_____

Who in your life have you stuck with like Ruth did Naomi?

_____

_____

_____

_____

_____

What does it mean to you to be accepted?

_____

_____

_____

_____

_____

Chapter Four
REGENERATION (I'VE BEEN REGENED!)

"You are what follows I Am"

~Joel Olsteen

I Am the woman naked on the roof. I Am the "jump off" that got pregnant the one time he jumped on. I Am the widow and the childless at the same time. Grieving from the murder of my husband and death of my child. Yes, he was murdered and now I Am the wife of the murderer. His boss killed him. I had nothing to do with it. I didn't ask for any of this. Nor did I do anything to deserve it. I Am Innocent. Why did this happen to me? How am I going to function in such dysfunction? Everyone expects me to move on. Somehow they promise this feeling will pass. What good can come out of this? I Am a Victim. Our marriage was born out of deception. Can God bless this? He can't bless this? I Am Punished. I was taken advantage of. I wasn't strong enough to fight him off. I have to tell my side, but I'm suffocating. I can't breathe. I Am Voiceless.

~ I Am Bathsheba

I gave Bathsheba a voice because many can identify with her. Some of us tried to help her while others simply ignored her. Well maybe not literally her, but that woman who *plays* the victim, *is* the victim, got caught up, and can't move on. The woman who feels like when it rains it pours. The woman who screams silently, *I cannot take one more thing*. She is on autopilot. She is living but not alive. Unfulfilled because of a lack of answers to mysteries in her life. Why did it happen? Why didn't it happen? Am I losing my mind? Did that really happen?

You don't wake up and get caught up in prostitution or drug addiction or even adultery. Not a woman on Earth plans for any of it. There is no way you mentally prepare for your child to die or your husband to leave because it was never in the blueprint. We all watched Cinderella and dreamed of the prince finding us and fitting us for the glass slipper. We all dreamed of having successful careers, loving marriages, raising great kids and living happily ever after.

In the book of Psalms, the descendants of Korah expressed profound despair, "I'm caught in a maze and can't find my way out, blinded by tears of pain and frustration." What sticks out to me in the verse is the word *blinded*. Understand, there is a "time" to mourn, but prolonged mourning invites grief and bitterness and those twins will have you sitting in your pit for a lifetime. The great thing about the pit is the only way out is up. The greater thing is Christ will come and sit in the pit with you, take your truth, give you His truth and pull you out. He will never abandon you there. The *only* thing He has ever abandoned is an empty grave and you should too. Stand up in the midst of your grave, your pit and wipe those tears that have blinded you from seeing your future. There is a better story line, Christ died for it, but you will never enjoy it replaying the past. He took care of that too. You didn't die. You're not dead.

I believe what you give your attention to becomes

your reality. The reason I don't look like what I have been through is because while what I have been through made me stronger and made me realize I was not built to break, I had to abandon every picture from my past that blinded me from becoming the woman Christ showed me when He gave me His truth. See, once my tears were wiped away, I saw something. A life weightier than the heaviness I was experiencing. I had to have it. Truth is, I already had it, but I would only see it as an unattainable dream. Until I woke up, got up, stood up and embraced the new life in front of me. Without always getting the answers I thought I needed to explain the unsolicited trauma that took place in my past. Somehow, it didn't matter anymore. Either way I had to say goodbye. It wasn't easy because if we are honest, we like to rock our pain. It's comfortable. Freedom from it requires action. Christ did *all* He is going to do. Now it's my turn.

Bathsheba got hers. After his process of repentance and restoration, she loved her some David. Her union to her husband produced a Solomon, the wisest man who ever lived. Through Solomon came our Savior, Jesus. Bathsheba was good with Bathsheba. She was happily married and went on to have eight children.

So how do you begin again? Establish yourself in a new truth that is concrete and not sand. Sand is comfortable.

Don't stay comfortable in your sorrow. The bible says, "...when you decree a thing it shall be established" (Job 22:28). Start by decreeing I Am Heard, I Am Redeemed, I Am Relentless, I Am Fierce, I Am Loved, I can see, Look at me, I'm Not That Woman, and run from there. You got this because He's got you!

My mission as a writer and speaker to women has a dual purpose. Number one is to uncover the *negative* core beliefs that govern your life and replace them with core beliefs founded upon your true identity and your value in God and Number two, to simply love the skin you are in.

Philemon 1:6 (New American Standard Bible, NASB), *And I pray that the fellowship of your faith may become effective through the knowledge of every good thing which is in you for Christ's sake.*

Many people are afraid to acknowledge the good things in them because they are worried it will be seen as arrogant or proud. But it is really acknowledging what Jesus has done for us. It is the secure women who are actually humble. False humility is the depreciation of our own godliness. We sometimes spend so much time dealing with what we don't like about ourselves. Too many people overvalue what they are not and undervalue what they are.

If our sense of identity is vague and uncertain, we can become subject to a storm-tossed existence in which external circumstances dictate our perspectives, our reactions and our decisions. Our identity must be rooted in truth. Low self-esteem leads to the development of a personality that excessively craves approval and affection and exhibits an extreme desire for personal achievement from an unhealthy place. To a person with low self-esteem, attention means approval and approval equals love. Just because someone shows you a little attention, you're in love.

The enemy tried it with me. Somehow at a young age, my crew was made up of white or light-skinned small girls with long hair. I was the darker girl with short hair.

70

Anytime we rolled to the mall or the fair in groups, all the guys would try to holler at one of my friends who was either light-skinned or white with pretty hair. In my pre-teen years I felt invisible because of this. Until it happened for me. Someone finally came for me. He was cute too. I was in love with the group "The Boys" back then and he looked like the oldest one named Kyrie. He was like, "Hey, girl." I was like, "Heyyyy," and instantly, I was in love.

I call it the ugly duckling syndrome. For the young girls reading this book, don't fall for it. Shoot, for the older ladies reading this book, don't fall for it. Just because ain't nobody looked your way in a long time don't mean the first one that turns his head or asks for your number is the one. I always tell women who are single, know who your husband is before he comes, so that when the counterfeit comes, you already know that's not it. This was important to me before I married. My desire was to get it right the first time and not to look at marriage as just dating, but a lifelong commitment. I had to abandon the thought in my subconscious that would say if it doesn't work out I can get out.

For me, divorce was not an option. With that being my position, I sought God early about my marriage covenant. There was this age-old argument about God giving us the ability and the liberty to choose a mate based on biblical criteria and the fairy tale, as some called it, of finding "the one" that God placed on this Earth for you. While I can argue both sides, my desire was to find the one. That was one fairy tale I was not willing to let go of. I wanted who God wanted for me. How did I know him before I met him? It was in knowing *Him*. I spent time asking God what my husband would be like. The bible says write the vision and

71

make it plain (Habakkuk 2:2). The more I spent time with God around it, the more He revealed to me who he was.

Did He give me his name, address and social security number? No. But I knew his nature, his character. I knew we were like minded and had like precious faith. I knew he had the same passion for God and the things of God that I had. I knew that our callings would complement each other. I knew being in his presence would feel a lot like the times God and I spent together. I would feel safe and wanted with butterflies in my stomach. I wrote everything down and locked it away, but I would take it out and read it every day. Honestly, while reading it I felt like my husband was there. He was. He was, at the time, my best friend, Demond. We met in church and spent a lot of time together as friends. But I remember the day I realized Demond was not just my friend but my husband.

He came over for a visit. But this visit was different. It had an urgency with it. He needed to tell me some things God spoke to him the day before. As he began to share, my heart literally melted. He began to reveal to me his vision for his life. What God had called him to do. He was so passionate. With tears in his eyes he said he just had to share with me. I sat there staring at him because everything he said I had written down as my vision for my husband, locked away in my file cabinet. Not wanting to reveal that to him, I simply said, "Let's pray." That was the first time I was in the presence of God so intimately with another person alongside me and it felt complete. This was him, my husband. Three weeks later on Valentine's Day he asked me to marry him. The rest is history, or should I say ourstory.

And even married women. You may be lacking attention at home. The devil will make sure he sends one of his boys to fill a void that you are missing in the house. He will come and compliment your hair, your clothing. Look too long. Talk too long. Everything about you to him is a 10. While you may have it like he likes it, remember the end of that is death. You need to stop leaving the house thirsty. Eat and drink at *home*. Yes, maybe your spouse is lacking in that area. My advice to you would be find a way to communicate that unmet need to him. But most importantly, get to the well where Jesus met the Samaritan woman and get some of the water that will cause you to never thirst again. The bible speaks of this plainly in II Timothy 3:1-4. The Silly woman is the modern day Thirsty woman. The bible says this woman will be prevalent in the last days. Don't be the woman that is unstable, needy because she attracts the wrong man whether she is married or not. This woman places affirmation in the wrong places. When we allow our frustrations and insecurities to lead us, we become the foolish woman. Don't be defined by a moment of foolishness.

I've talked to Job's wife about that. Take a listen:

A Foolish Moment

What my husband really said was, "You don't sound like yourself." What you read in Job Chapter 2 is "You speak <u>as</u> one of the foolish women." And when you read that in our story, you place me in your "foolish" woman hall of fame. In a moment of weakness I said something foolish. Looking at my husband's sores on his body while cleaning the pus that ran down his skin made me angry. Was it not hard enough to be hurting inside, but to be in constant agonizing physi-

73

cal pain as well pissed me off. Losing my children made me feel helpless and ashamed. I lost more breath at every thought of it. I was dying inside. These thoughts and feelings filled me. I surrendered to the pain and for a moment let it consume me. It irritated me to sit there and listen to him still speak positively. I was pissed and in my feelings, to say the least. So I said something in that moment that I am remembered for, "Curse God and die!" (Job 2:9)

I was there beside him through it all. It was a difficult season that most don't make it through. You gasp as you read those words as if you have never said them— well maybe not out loud. You have been "in your feelings" too, and some of you have entertained the possibility of suspending your belief in God and ending your relationship with Him. Especially when you think He authored a tragedy in your life. He doesn't do that. He is a good Father who often gets blamed for things He did not do. Thank God neither He nor Job held my feelings against me. God restored everything. My womb even lived again; I had 10 more children. See, I stayed through the tragedy and was able to take part in the victory. Victory always exceeds tragedy. We received double for our shame. Don't allow your entire existence to be defined by a foolish moment. Keep people around you who see the real you and keep you encouraged.

Thank God my husband was able to look at me and say, "You're Not That Woman!" And this is what I am saying to you today—Woman, Don't Be a Fool!

~Job's wife

The bible says that a fool says in his heart there is no God (Psalm 14:1). What is in your heart will eventually come out of your mouth. We see this clearly with Job's wife. Ask yourself what lurks on the bottom floor of your soul that may cause you to say, think, or do foolish things. In Proverbs Chapter 4:23 we are warned to guard our hearts because out of it flow the issues of life. Many times we have "issues" because we have not guarded our hearts against negativity that is produced out of disappointment and disappointment drains you. It drains you of all things good and when that happens, here come foolish words and ways. Being a foolish woman causes you to be unprepared when it's your season. Just ask the five foolish virgins. Foolish women tear things down with their bare hands, particularly their homes according to Proverbs. Foolish people are easily tricked. Ask the Galatians. Don't be the modern day foolish woman and go slit someone's tires because they got out on you. Just move on. You'd be a fool not to sleep with your husband as punishment. That's just dumb. And ladies, please stop saying foolish things that call for labels that God never placed on you. You don't want to go in the foolish woman hall of fame.

Listen, God is never surprised by disappointment. But normally when you are severely disappointed it's because you are longing for something greater than Him. God is our greatest good and knowing Him is the highest satisfaction man can ever have. Psalm 16:2 says, "You are my Lord. My welfare has no existence outside of you." Wow, that literally sent chills down my arm. In this life things may happen, but with Him you will see the victory. The greatest reward is Him and navigating through disappointment with Him, you are sure to receive double.

If I honestly had to sum up my mission in life, it would

be helping people discover who they are.

One of the greatest enemies plaguing our generation is identity. In discovering who we are, it is important to know our history. Everyone wants to know where they come from. Who they really are. When you have an illness, be it physical or mental, you see a doctor. It is aggressively taught in the medical field that the diagnosis is revealed through the patient's history. They believe your history or where you come from can help diagnose your present and ultimately your destiny. Mama and "them" had cancer, so according to their calculations, there is a probability that you will too. Mama and "them" suffered from bipolar disorder, so there is a chance you will as well. And to be totally honest, it's true. You can look in a person's history and tell them who they are and who they will be.

Scientists say you are a product of genetic determinism (DNA). If your natural parents are tall then you will be tall. Then there is environmental determinism which says you will be a product of your environment. The environment around you will determine who you will be.

During sex, all that was in your mother's soul and all that was in your father's soul [his soul was wrapped up in that seed (sperm)] came together and produced you. Now some of our parents may not have known how to break generational curses, so consequently the things they may not have dealt with got passed down to you and so I will say some things you deal with in life may not be your fault (ex. depression, oppression, bad attitude, and low self-image), but it is time for you to take responsibility. You can blame people all your life for why you are the way you are, but until you take responsibility and decide to change, you will stay that way.

1 John 5:18 tells us that we are born of God. Literally God is our father. You need to wake up every day and remind yourself that you are God's child. I know you may have your earthly father's last name, but you have been stamped with your heavenly Father's identity. While your earthly father's sperm may have produced some genetics that can cause some issues, not your heavenly Father. In 1 Peter 1:23 (AMP) it reads,

23 You have been regenerated (born again), not from a mortal origin (seed, sperm), but from one that is immortal by the ever living and lasting Word of God.

Which means God's seed has no imperfections. See, your father's seed may have produced an imperfect child, but when you were born again you became incorruptible. You have to identify with your new birth, not your first birth.

And the best of all. The scripture that should be tattooed on all of our foreheads in case we get amnesia is 2 Corinthians 5:17,

17 Therefore if any man be in Christ, he is a new creature: old things are passed away; behold, all things are become new.

Either I am new, or I am not. Either old things have passed away or they have not. If I am new, I am not conducting myself like that old. I am not referring to the old when the situation seems more favorable to do so. We have to stop playing double dutch between the old and the new. You are in Christ. Your identity is in Christ. So here is the best news of the day. If you do not like the way you were born the first time, you can be *born again* (re-fathered, re-gened)! Some of you just need to be born again and walk in the reality of your new birth.

As far as environmental determinism, which says you are a product of your environment, Philippians 3:20, (AMP) tells us,

[20]But [we are different, because] our citizenship is in heaven. And from there we eagerly await [the coming of] the Savior, the Lord Jesus Christ;

Your homeland is heaven! That is the environment you carry.

So in summation you have to stop allowing your history, which no longer exists, define you. God can deliver you from trauma and the memory of it. God is an eternal God. He can step into your past and heal you so that you no longer feel the effects of the trauma. Many times we like to wear our trauma as a badge of honor or a blanket. We like for it to comfort us and define us, hindering the work of the Holy Spirit in your life. But God wants to deliver you from trauma and heal you from the effects of it.

My husband and I have both experienced this first-hand. Knowing that God is an eternal God, who doesn't exist in time, we believe He can step from the present and heal us of our past. Especially the story that is robbing you of your destiny.

My husband and I have been pastoring in Southern Maryland for some time now and during a particular graduation season we decided to support as many of our graduates as we could. In order to do this, we had to divide to multiply. He attended some and I attended others. He found himself at a graduation where someone who had abused him was attending. He was abused sexually from age 4-7 and was never able to fully disclose the details of what happened because he was a boy. "Boys don't get abused sexually," he was told. As he stood in complete stillness staring at this woman coming towards him with her arms wide open to receive affection and acceptance that she obviously did not deserve, he became that little boy again. All the fear, shame and inadequacy were present. Here he was almost 40 but felt 4. He was paralyzed.

The moment she hugged him he was instantly taken back to the place where he would get abused and God stepped in and healed him. Healing took place in a moment and when he opened his eyes as they were embracing, he could now see her through God's eyes. God stepped into eternity and healed him of his past. This happened in a matter of moments. It was supernatural.

Sometimes we don't understand why we have the behaviors we have. I have learned what God reveals in our lives He wants to heal. I had been pastoring for about two years when I came upon times when requests for me to speak at conferences and MC events increased. Many requests were coming from organizations I was not familiar with. On the inside I felt weird, kinda awkward and unyielding to even pray about it. I would say things like, "Why do they want me?" or "I'm not sure I want to take it." This was coming from an insecure place in me that I personally thought I had overcome. My husband would say to me, "Why *not* you?" He encouraged me to pray, not about the engagements, but about why I felt the way I did.

One day I decided to do just that. In my time of prayer I had an open vision. I was in the back seat of my late grandmother's car. It was as if I were in a scene of the movie *Scrooged,* where I could see something that happened in the past, but they could not see me. In the front seat was my grandmother and an about eight-year-old Portia. I was noticeably upset. I asked my grandmother why my sister got to go with a couple and I had to stay with her. My grandmother looked at little Portia and in her sweet, yet impressionable voice she said, "Because Nikkie is pretty. People like to flaunt her around." Now my grandmother did not say I wasn't pretty, but that is what I understood. I watched little Portia have a moment of impact that would negatively affect her view of herself for years to come.

As I was watching, something rose up on the inside of me. That was such a lie! So much so I began to laugh, and I mean uncontrollably. I thought it was hilarious that I would even think I was not good enough for anyone to choose me. That laughter turned into a cleansing cry and I felt God's presence there with me. He was healing me right in that moment while revealing to me why my behavior did not line up with my true identity. Like my husband, I was healed in a moment. I was no longer the woman who didn't think she was good enough. I am the woman who has a word in my mouth for my generation and generations to come. I carry something unique called truth that exposes and diminishes the lies the enemy still tries to whisper in women's ears. I am a woman sought after and needed. I've been regened. Oh, and I am cute too☺.

Reflections

What have you allowed in your history to show up in to-day's reality

_____

_____

_____

What haven't you done because of fear?

_____

_____

_____

List the differences between your new birth and your first birth.

_____

_____

_____

_____

Chapter Five
DEATH BECOMES HER

I guess I was about 16 years old when we discovered her appearing to be lifeless on the floor. My sister, myself and two cousins had been hanging out in our basement and as it got later in the evening, we needed more light in the recreation room. My sister instructed my cousin Dawn, to go get her lamp out of the room. As Dawn was wrestling to pull the plug out of the makeshift socket my uncle had created (my sister's room was an unfinished part of the basement and it had just been finished), she was electrocuted. The power throughout the entire house blinked and we heard a loud thump that we quickly realized was my cousin's body dropping to the hard concrete floor.

We all stood over her body, screaming her name, *"Dawn! Dawn!"* No one wanted to touch her, fearing we too would die. My heart sank; I let out one last scream of her name, *"Dawwwwn!"* *She answered, "Yes, Lord."* My sister leaned down to give her a hand up and said, *"Girl, you are still here on Earth...get up!"* We all gasped for any air we could find after holding our breath in disbelief for so long. Those couple of minutes seemed like hours. One thing I will say, she played dead well.

Death does strange, yet interesting things to people. Obviously, there are many emotions involved when someone passes, but eventually there is an emotional transition. We come to a place of peace with death because we make statements like, "They are in a better place," or "They are finally at peace." Well, I remember the day I died. If death means passing from one bad place to enter a better one, if it means finally resting in peace, then I died. It happened at an altar when my lifeless body fell to the ground from the disappointments of my world, I was tired, so I unplugged. I took the power source away from this place, this unfinished closed-in room that I could hardly breathe in that kept telling me I would not make it. I didn't make it. I died right in my Father's arms and truly woke up on the other side with a "Yes, Lord."

Isn't that what we all did? Or did you? Maybe you got it twisted when you read what the bible says, "Old things are passed away, behold all things are new." The problem with most people is that they have never experienced the reality of death in their walk with God. They never have had an authentic *Yes, Lord*—an entrance into the new. See, to die is gain. When you die *in Him,* your past has passed away. Your days of trying to make it work on your own have passed. Your traumatic history as a victim has passed. Your inability to make right choices has passed. Even your old DNA has died, and you have been regened. You have the DNA of your Father. You are just like Him. With that in mind, stop playing the role of a character that no longer exists. Role play makes you and others believe you are someone you are not. Trust me, I know that old woman tries to resurrect, but *you're not that woman!* Be the woman who defeated terror, guilt and disappointment because you really did. Don't *play* dead well. *Be* dead well.

The reality of you being in Christ has to be more than just a scripture or a story. Your past will come for you. It will call for you when it's convenient and comfortable. Literally like a booty call. It's like that dude who texts at 3 a.m. and asks what you're doing and memories you know weren't all that, suddenly become appealing again because you feel a void you think he can fill.

Who and what you used to be always seems to creep back up as if they were the best times of your life. You hear an old song and it triggers a memory and your mouth gets involved with the thought, "Girl, I remember when..." There is something about those '90s that has us who are 45 and older reliving them constantly. It was the best music, the best clothes, the best movies that had the best dances and clothes in them. But we rehearse the '90s as if good times only existed with that decade. I no longer focus on this being my year, but my new confession is this is my *decade*.

Every day tell yourself there is something new for you. Find your life in Christ.

Do not remember the former things, Now it shall spring forth;

Shall you not know it [Isaiah 43:18-19, New King James Version (NKJV)]?

I believe there is nothing wasted in God's Kingdom. God has the right and the ability to use everything you have been through for your good and for His glory. Many of you, like me, have such an awesome testimony of deliverance and freedom. I encourage you to share it. Tell it to women who are still stuck. But you are not what you have been through. You have to live with the reality that your past has passed away. The bible encourages us not to even remember them. He is doing a new thing—*now*. You cannot hold on to the old and reach for the new at the same time. The apostle Paul tells us this in Philippians 3:13 (New Living Translation),

No, dear brothers and sisters, I have not achieved it, but I focus on this one thing; forgetting the past and looking forward to what lies ahead.

You cannot remember and look forward at the same time. You have to abandon one to do the other. The New International Version says *straining* toward what lies ahead. When I read that I get a picture of an outstretch neck. An expectation. An effort to push into something new. There are new possibilities in your life in Christ.

Personally, there are many daily practices I have for attaining and living in who I am. One I like to call feeding and starving. I understand that you are always feeding. Your inner man, your soul is always receiving. I understand that whatever you feed is going to grow and what you don't feed will die. Daily I starve every insecurity that comes to rob me of my new identity. I starve every past failure. When the enemy tries to give me a past memory, I remind him it is under the blood, cast it down and replace it with the new information I received as a new woman. There are some things you have to literally starve to *death*. Don't feed your history. Don't re-live your past. You may ask, "How do you feed?" By declaring and receiving new information. Remember how Eve was able to carry out a vision that was never meant for her? She received a seed. She saw what the serpent said. A thought was planted, and her mouth got involved. Well, duh... let's try that with the word.

Meditation

Meditation is the key to your new identity. I think it is funny how every religion has the practice of mediation. They understand its importance. There is a difference with biblical meditation. Many people practice Eastern meditation, which is the emptying of your mind. It is a clearing of space. That's all good, but for our new life in Christ, we have to put something in. We have to feed. We need it to go deep. We have to meditate on the word of God. That is the seed we need to birth our new life in Christ. Meditation means to coo; mutter, to speak out loud, a deep reflective thought, to roll over in your thinking, to look at something for a long time. To contemplate, to stare. You have to stare at new possibilities. Roll over in your thinking your new identity. Give thought to the word of God. To meditate is to chew on something, like a cow chewing on grass and then bringing it back up again and chewing it again. And then speak it. C'mon, ladies, you know how to run your mouth. Well, take the word and get to talking.

Joshua, who is truly my prototype, was a different type of leader. Moses was gone and while Moses led the people out of Egypt into the wilderness, he never made it to the Promised Land. I believe it was because the people kept looking back. They talked about how they missed the bondages they were in. They even said things like, "I wish I would have died in Egypt." I believe they said those things because they did not have a reality of the Promised Land.

They could see it but not possess it because they were saying the wrong things. They were practicing the negative form of meditation—*worry*. Worry will rob you of the new. Worry is simply rehearsing the old. We worry about stupid stuff that isn't even real. But because we meditate on it and then give voice to it, that thing we worry about now becomes real. We have creative power. We have to learn how to create the new.

Now we have Joshua as a new leader. I love how his story begins, *Moses my servant is dead, now therefore arise*. Arise, meaning to change your posture and your position. Arise, meaning to get up from where you are. Joshua had to arise and change in order for his life to produce something new. He was a beast of a leader and you are too. But the key to him possessing everything God had for him was meditation. The bible says in Joshua 1:8 (NKJV),

This book of the law shall not depart from your mouth; but you shall mediate in it day and night that you may observe to do according to all that is written in it. For then you will make your way prosperous, and then you will have good success.

This is a recipe for a new life. Be strong, be courageous.

Have the audacity to be who God called you to be. Arise from every pit this world has you in. Meditate on that word day and night and you will make yourself prosperous and you will have good success.

I realize it takes courage to die. Death will always precede a new life. It's something Lot's wife talks to me about often. She wouldn't die *to* the old and instead she died *in* the old. Let's listen in on a conversation with her:

You hear about me and you ask, "Why did she look back?" My answer is pretty simple: the same reason you do. Looking back was the last step before my death. It began with lingering. I wasn't just afraid of what was before me, it was what I would have to give up to obtain it. That is why I lingered. They came to rescue me from my home. A place I thought was my refuge. That is why I did not want to participate in the rescue. God sent them to lead me out of a place that was destined for destruction, but it was a comfortable place for me. I'd made a life there, that's why I lingered.

As they were snatching me out of my comfort zone and pulling me up this mountain, I would catch glimpses of what I thought were the best times in life. I had my children there. Two of my daughters were married there. I wasn't ready to leave and this mountain we had to go up to get to where they said we would now reside, it was hard to climb. It was a higher place, but would I survive there? Would the elevation choke me because I could not breathe at that altitude, in that atmosphere? It was raining fire and brimstone that day in my city, but somehow, I thought I could still function in that atmosphere.

I became used to functioning in dysfunction. They were sprinting, I was speed walking...lingering. I could not bring anything with me. I would not need anything from that old place.

They said to flee to the mountain, charging me to move quickly at maximum speed, but I could not see where we were headed, that's why I lingered. If I am being honest with you, this place was all I knew, and they were telling me it would no longer exist. To stay would mean the end of my existence. I didn't believe them and that's why I lingered. So you ask me why I looked back, I ask you the same question. Why do you linger when it is time for you to move in life? You too look back and when you do, you will become immobile, stuck, lifeless, a memorial for others to look at and say, "Could she not see there was better?" There is better.

My name is Idit and I am a native of Sodom. I was born there, and I grew up there. My entire life and legacy was defined by one sentence in the bible, "His wife looked back from behind him, and she became a pillar of salt." My name was never mentioned.

~Lot's wife

Many people look back because they cannot see what is ahead. I often tell people to close their eyes to see. It's when our eyes are open that we look too long at the obstacles that are hindering us from moving. But when we close our eyes and allow God to capture our imagination, we then realize that nothing is impossible. Lot's wife would tell you to close your eyes and run when those doors of opportunity are opened to you. She would tell you to follow the map that is provided in your mind's eye instead of the obstacle course you see when your physical eyes are open. She would explain to you that there are always angelic forces ahead of you, paving the way that God ordained for you and if you don't look back, their hand is right there to pull you forward.

That mountain she had to climb was symbolic of "pulling up," something else I often tell women. Don't allow your comfortability to lie to you and hold you down. A recipe for not looking back is to pull up and don't linger. Don't linger in wrong relationships that you know God is calling you out of. When you get out, don't look back. When your past calls and says, "Hello from the other side," your answer should be, "*This* side no longer requires you," then *Hang Up!*

Don't linger in humanity's controls that keep you enslaved. You don't need anyone's permission to be free. Don't linger in environments that have blinded you from seeing new places. When you are tempted to pick back up the old weights of depression, frustration, loneliness and rejection you dropped while climbing that mountain, let them know that where you are headed, you no longer require them. Sweetie, it's a new season and it's time to get up that mountain. You don't need to *look back* to tell the old *I Am Not That Woman!* Scream it as you move forward!

I Am Right

For our sake he made him to be sin who knew no sin, so that in him we might be made the righteousness of God in him (2 Corinthians 5:21 ESV).

In our sin nature we are always wrong. The enemy is always trying to tell you that you are wrong. But Christ died to make you right. You have to declare, I am the righteousness of God in Christ Jesus! Not because of anything I have done but because of what Christ did for me. The bible says in Isaiah 54:14 that you are established in righteousness. Established is concrete. Like your name is written in concrete, never to be erased. We cannot come in and out of our righteousness! Just like we cannot be unborn. You can die, but you cannot be unborn (established). You are in Christ! When you live anything outside of that, you are being inauthentic. Even when we do sin, the Spirit convicts us by reminding us of our righteousness. You don't have to live by your past experience but His past victory! Your past has been erased.

Who hath delivered us from the power of darkness and hath translated us unto the kingdom of his dear son

(Colossians 1:13).

We can no longer access something that is not there. Everything we do has to come from a position of being *in Christ!*

You cannot go back and undo your past, but Christ erased it and gave you a *new* past. You not only get a new future but a new past. We think like Christ is in us, but we have to think like we are in Him. His life is our life. So with reality we can create something new. We are co-creators with God. Every day we can walk in our new identity and declare a new possibility. A new way of living.

I titled this book *I'M NOT THAT WOMAN* in hopes of pointing you to who you are. You will only discover that by looking at Christ. Your life is hidden in Him.

If your first concern is to look after yourself, you'll never find yourself. But if you forget about yourself and look to me, you'll find both yourself and me (Matthew 10:39 MSG).

God is a master planner. He already planned and prearranged a good life for you before the foundation of the world. Your born-again experience was already mapped out. You just have to get on the path.

For we are His workmanship [his own masterwork], a work of art], created in Christ Jesus [reborn from above— spiritually transformed, renewed, ready to be used] for good works, which God prepared [for us] beforehand [taking paths which he set], so that we would walk in them [living the good life which He prearranged and made ready for us] (Ephesians 2:10 AMP).

I have spent time telling you who you are not. But I want you to spend the rest of your time declaring who you are. I will get you started with I Am confessions. Say them every day. I'm so happy that you aren't that woman anymore, now let's see who you really are.

Love you,

Portia Taylor

I AM CONFESSIONS

I AM GOD'S CHILD – Romans 8:16

I AM JUSTIFIED. JUST AS IF I'D NEVER SINNED –Romans 5:1

I AM A NEW WOMAN – 2 Corinthians 5:17 I HAVE MY DAD'S NATURE – 2 Peter 1:4

I AM A STRONG WOMAN – Ephesians 6:10

I AM A KEPT WOMAN – 1 Peter 1:5

I AM AN OVERCOMER – 1 John 4:4

I AM AN HEIR OF GOD – Romans 8:17

I AM EMPOWERED TO PROSPER – Deuteronomy 8:7

I AM A HEALED WOMAN – 1 Peter 2:24

I AM A CONQUERING WOMAN – Romans 8:37

I AM A WOMAN OF FAITH – 2 Corinthians 4:18

I AM A RIGHTEOUS WOMAN – 2 Corinthians 5:21

I AM A WOMAN OF LIGHT– Matthew 5:14

I AM FORGIVEN – Colossians 1:13-14

I AM REDEEMED – Psalms 107:2

I AM STABLE – 2 Corinthians 4:18

I AM SANCTIFIED – 1 Corinthians 6:11

I AM GOD'S OWN HANDIWORK – Ephesians 2:10

I AM FEARLESS – 2 Timothy 1:7

I AM FAITHFUL – Romans 12:3

I AM WEALTHY – Psalms 112:3

I AM HEALTHY – Proverbs 4:20-23

I AM COMPLETE – Colossians 2:10

I AM EXTRAORDINARY – Luke 1:37

I AM A WISE WOMAN-Proverbs 14:1

I AM BEAUTIFUL-Psalms 139:14

I AM LOVED-I John 4:10

I AM CONFIDENT-Philippians 4:13

I AM STRONG-Isaiah 41:10

I AM FEARLESS: Psalm 118:6

I AM WOMAN

Reflections

Write some of your own **I AM** confessions to declare every day.

_____

_____

_____

_____

_____

What does it mean to you to be righteous?

_____

_____

_____

_____

_____

What needs to die in you?

_____

_____

_____

_____

_____

_____

_____

_____

ABOUT THE AUTHOR

Portia Taylor pastors Victory Christian Ministries International Charles County alongside her husband, Demond Taylor. Together, they are extending the vision of Apostles Tony and Cynthia Brazelton into Southern Maryland where they teach the word of God with boldness and clarity to a multicultural church.

Pastor Portia has empowered thousands of women with her "I'm Not That Woman" message, a revelation God gave her years ago as she studied various women in the Bible, from those who were praised to those who were marginalized.

Armed with the love of God and a no-nonsense approach, her primary goals are to lead people to understanding their true identity in Jesus Christ, empower women, and help them walk in the freedom that God has given them.

Portia Taylor

www.portiataylor.com

CPSIA information can be obtained
at www.ICGtesting.com
Printed in the USA
FFHW02n1910071018
48696407-52723FF